Mayan Temple
At Tikal

FACES
AND
PLACES

GUATEMALA

BY ELMA SCHEMENAUER

THE CHILD'S WORLD®, INC.

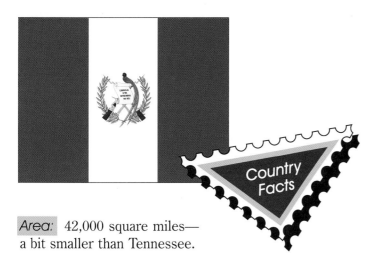

Country Facts

Area: 42,000 square miles—
a bit smaller than Tennessee.

Population: About 11 million people.

Capital City: Guatemala City.

Other Important Cities: Quetzaltenango, Escuintla, Puerto Barrios,
and Antigua.

Money: The quetzal. A quetzal is divided into 100 centavos.

National Bird: The quetzal.

National Flag: A flag with three stripes: two blue and one white. On the white
band is a coat of arms. It includes a quetzal (the national bird), the
date of independence, two crossed rifles, and two crossed swords.

National Song: "Himno Nacional," or "National Hymn."

National Holiday: Independence Day on September 15.

Head of Government: The president of Guatemala.

Text copyright © 1999 by The Child's World®, Inc.
All rights reserved. No part of this book may be reproduced
or utilized in any form or by any means without written
permission from the publisher.
Printed in the United States of America.

Library of Congress Cataloging-in-Publication Data
Schemenauer, Elma.
Guatemala / by Elma Schemenauer.
Series: "Faces and Places".
p. cm.
Includes index.
Summary: Describes the location, people, food, plants and
animals, customs, and other aspects of the country of Guatemala
ISBN 1-56766-578-0 (library : reinforced : alk. paper)

1. Guatemala — Juvenile literature.
[1. Guatemala.] I. Title.

F1463.2.S44 1999
972.81 — dc21

98-37080
CIP
AC

GRAPHIC DESIGN
Robert A. Honey, Seattle

PHOTO RESEARCH
James R. Rothaus / James R. Rothaus & Associates

ELECTRONIC PRE–PRESS PRODUCTION
Robert E. Bonaker / Graphic Design & Consulting Co.

PHOTOGRAPHY
Cover photo: Young Guatemalan Girl
By Dave G. Houser/Corbis

Table of Contents

What if you were a giant bird soaring high over Earth? You would see huge land areas with water around them. These land areas are called **continents**. Some continents are made up of several countries. The United States and Mexico are on the continent of North America. So is the Republic of Guatemala.

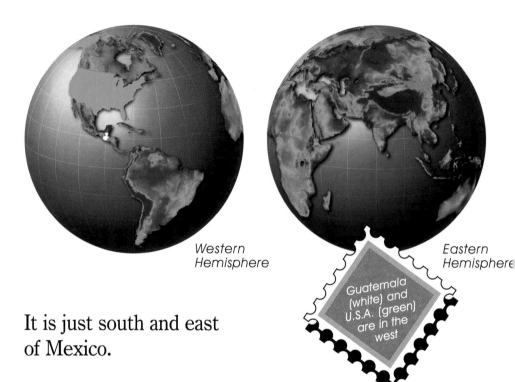

Western Hemisphere

Eastern Hemisphere

Guatemala (white) and U.S.A. (green) are in the west

It is just south and east of Mexico.

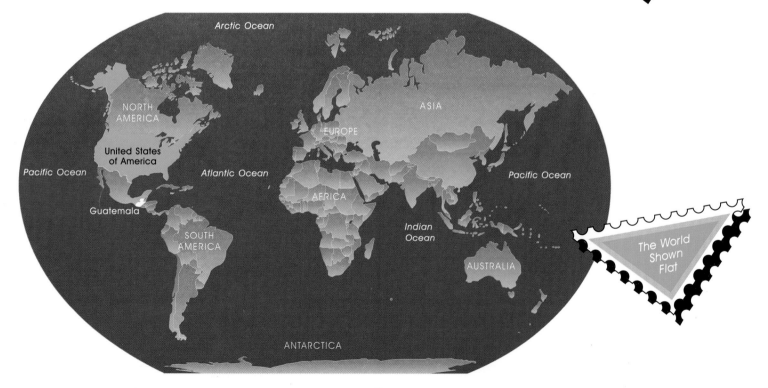

Arctic Ocean

NORTH AMERICA

United States of America

ASIA

EUROPE

Pacific Ocean

Atlantic Ocean

AFRICA

Pacific Ocean

Guatemala

SOUTH AMERICA

Indian Ocean

AUSTRALIA

ANTARCTICA

The World Shown Flat

6

Gulf of
Mexico

MEXICO

BELIZE

Atlantic
Ocean

GUATEMALA

HONDURAS

EL SALVADOR

NICARAGUA

Pacific
Ocean

COSTA RICA

Close-Up
of
Guatemala

Volcanoes
And
Farmland
In The
Highlands
Near Patzun

Tikal

Flores

PÉTEN

CARIBBEAN LOWLAND

HIGHLANDS

Patzun

PACIFIC LOWLAND

The Purcell Team/Corbis

Guatemala has four land areas. The hot, swampy *Pacific lowland* runs along the Pacific coast of the country. Closer to the middle of Guatemala are the *highlands*. The highlands are made up of mountains and high plains. The highlands have cool weather and good soil. Most Guatemalans live in the highlands.

Jungle Surrounds Mayan City Ruins At Tikal

Charles & Josette Lenars/Corbis

Large Lily Pads Cover A Swamp Near Flores

Along the Caribbean coast of the country is the *Caribbean lowland*. Like the Pacific lowland, it is hot and swampy. A warm plain is north of Guatemala's other land areas. This is called the *Péten*.

Wind Blows Palm Trees Along The Caribbean Coast

Paolo Ragazzini/Corbis

Reinhard Eisele/Corbis

Keel-Billed Toucan From Péten

Kevin Schafer/Corbis

Grasses and trees grow in the Pacific lowland, but many have been cleared for farming. In the highlands, trees such as oak, cedar, cypress, and rosewood grow. Rain forests cover both the Caribbean Lowland and the Péten.

Giant Cypress Tree At Tikal

Dave G. Houser/Corbis

Guatemala's animals include deer, coyotes, monkeys, pumas, armadillos, and crocodiles. Birds such as parrots and toucans live in Guatemala, too. A bright green and red bird called the *quetzal* is the national bird of Guatemala. Sadly, not many quetzals are left in the wild. To save them, Guatemalans are working to keep them from dying.

Rare Female Quetzal Perching Outside Nest

Natalie Fobes/Corbis

Tikal

PÉTEN

CARIBBEAN
LOWLAND

PACIFIC
LOWLAND

Closeup
Of Guatemalan
Ocelot

Maya Ruins
At Tikal

Tikal ∴
PÉTEN

Mask Of Pedro de Alvarado

Long ago, a group of people called the *Maya* built palaces and pyramids in the warm Péten region. They used a form of picture writing, and were good at mathematics. When explorers from the country of Spain arrived, they found Mayans growing corn and other crops in the highlands.

Charles & Josette Lenars/Corbis

Picture Writing On A Monument At Tikal

Charles & Josette Lenars/Corbis

In 1524, a Spanish leader named Pedro de Alvarado took over what is now Guatemala. The country of Spain ruled Guatemala until 1821. Since then, many people have fought over who should rule the country.

Mask of Tecumuman, Last Mayan Emperor

Charles & Josette Lenars/Corbis

Guatemala Today

For a number of years, different leaders fought a lot about what kind of government Guatemala should have. Many Guatemalans lost their homes, or were hurt or killed when they got caught in these fights. Some fled to other countries to get away from the fighting.

In 1996 Guatemalan leaders signed a peace agreement. Guatemalans and other people around the world hope the country will learn to live in peace.

Charles & Josette Lenars/Corbis

In 1982 These Military Officers Took Power

Border Between Honduras And Guatemala

UPI/Corbis-Bettman

Guatemala City ☆ HONDURAS BORDER

Guatemala's National Palace

Dave G. Houser/Corbis

People Gathering At A Market In El Tejar

Chichicastenango • El Tejar • Jocotan
Antigua

The Purcell Team/Corbis

The People

More than 11 million people live in Guatemala. Nearly half are Maya Indians. Many others have both Mayan and Spanish relatives. They are called **ladinos**.

There are many differences between Mayans and ladinos. Mayans speak Indian languages, wear colorful clothes, and often live in country villages. Ladinos speak Spanish, follow Spanish and American ways, and often live in towns and cities.

Galen Rowell/Corbis

Young Lady From Chichicastenango

Buddy Mays/Corbis

Ladino Resting Near Antigua Market Square

Mayan Family From Jocotan

Richard A. Cooke/Corbis

City Life
And
Country
Life

ADMIT ONE ADMIT ONE

Guatemala's cities are a lot like cities in the Untied States. There are busy streets and big buildings. There are stores and hotels, too. If they have enough money, city families live in big houses and shop in fancy stores.

Family Homes In Flores

Dave G. Houser/Corbis

But many city people are poor. Some must live in tiny shacks. In country villages, most families live in small houses built of sun-dried bricks. These houses sometimes have dirt floors and tin roofs.

Cities, towns, and country villages all have weekly markets. There, people gather to make deals for beans, avocados, chickens, eggs, handmade toys, pottery, masks, brightly woven blankets, and other goods.

Decorated Photographic Store In Huehuetenango

Jeremy Horner/Corbis

A Rich Family Home In Chichicastenango

Charles & Josette Lenars/Corbis

Flores
•

Huehuetenango •

• Chichicastenango

Lake Atitlan

A Village
And Volcano
On
Lake Atitlan

Teacher
And Children
In School
At Lake
Atitlan

Lake
Atitlan
•Antigua

Jack Fields/Corbis

The University Of San Carlo Barromes In Antigua

Charles & Josette Lenars/Corbis

Guatemalan law says all children must go to school from age seven to 14. In the cities, most do. But in the country, there are not enough schools. Some country children never have a chance to go to school.

Having Class Outdoors On A Nice Day

Arvind Garg/Corbis

Spanish is Guatemala's main language. It was brought over by the Spanish explorers. About 20 Indian languages are also spoken in Guatemala. The most common is a Mayan language called *Queché*. (kay–CHAY) Many Indians speak their own Indian language even if they can also speak Spanish.

Work

In the country many people work on huge farms called **plantations**. Sugar cane, coffee beans, bananas, and corn are all grown on Guatemalan plantations. Rubber, cotton, rice, and other crops are grown there, too. In the cities, Guatemalans do the same kinds of jobs as Americans do. They work in banks, stores, offices, and trucking companies.

Some Guatemalans also work in a job called **tourism**. In this job, Guatemalans show visitors around their country. They show them the ruins of beautiful old Mayan buildings in the Péten.

Bagging Coffee Beans In San Pedro

Owen Franken/Corbis

Workers At Guatemala City's Telephone Exchange

Mayan Girl Sells Woven Wallets In Antigua

Dave Bartruff/Corbis

Enzo Ragazzini/Corbis

PÉTEN

Lake
Atitlan
• ☆ Guatemala City
Antigua

San Pedro •

Tourist Boat
Docked On
Lake Atitlan

Open Air
Market In
Chichicastenango

Puerto Barrios

Chichicastenango
Solola
☆ Guatemala City

Craig Lovell/Corbis

Food

For Mayans of long ago, corn was an important food. It is still important in Guatemala. People make corn pancakes called **tortillas** and wrap these around beans, rice, or other foods. Guatemalans also like to eat vegetables and fruits such as peppers, cabbage, celery, tomatoes, bananas, mangos, and pineapples. They also enjoy eggs.

Many Guatemalans are too poor to eat meat— except on special days. When a holiday or other special day comes, many people eat chicken or beef. Along the coasts, many families enjoy dishes made with fish such as tuna and snapper.

Arvind Garg/Corbis

Guatemala City Woman Preparing Fry Bread

Paolo Ragazzini/Corbis

Butcher's Shop In Solola

Sacks Of Seeds And Spices In Puerto Barrios

Jeremy Horner/Corbis

Guatemalan city people enjoy sports such as soccer, cycling, and basketball. Many do not have TV at home, so they often go to restaurants or other places in town to watch TV with their friends. They also like dancing and attending concerts and plays.

For country people, the main pastimes are religious festivals, or **fiestas** (fee–YES–tas). The fiestas are often a mixture of old and new ways and ideas. They include parades, games, fireworks, music, and dancing.

Dancers In The Nahuala Market

Nick Wheeler/Corbis

Guatemalan Girls' Basketball Group

Arvind Garg/Corbis

Horse Race In Todos Santos

Nik Wheeler/Corbis

The Purcell Team/Corbis

Todos Santos

Nahuala

Antigua

Small
Sailboat
In Antigua

All Saints'
Day Festival
In
Todos Santos

Todos Santos

Izabal

Antigua

Holidays

ADMIT ONE   ADMIT ONE

Every village, town, and city in Guatemala has its own fiestas. The whole country celebrates other holidays, too. Christmas, Easter, and All Saints Day are holidays that all Guatemalans celebrate together.

Child Dressed As Easter Bunny In Izabal

Colored Sawdust Carpet For Catholic Festival In Antigua

Charles & Josette Lenars/Corbis

Arvind Garg/Corbis

Guatemala is a land of old ways and new ideas. Perhaps one day you will get the chance to see this beautiful country. If you do, see if you can spot all the places and things you have just learned about in this book!

Detail Of
Mayan
Funerary
Vessel

Guatemala is known for its **marimba** music. A marimba, like a xylophone, has bars of different sizes. People tap these bars with small hammers to make beautiful music.

In the Péten region, people gather sap from a certain kind of evergreen tree. This sap, called chicle (CHEE–klay) is sold to make chewing gum.

Earthquakes sometimes shake the highlands region. This region also has many volcanoes. From time to time, some let off steam. In some areas, volcanic ash has made the soil very rich.

Since most Guatemalans do not own cars, many travel by bus. The cheaper buses are called "chicken buses." That is because people use them to take live chickens and other goods to market.

How Do You Say?

English	SPANISH	HOW TO SAY IT
Hello	hola	(OH-la)
Goodbye	hasta luego	(AH-stuh loo-AY-goh)
Please	por favor	(POR fah-VOR)
Thank You	gracias	(GRA-see-uss)
One	uno	(OO-no)
Two	dos	(DOHS)
Three	tres	(TRACE)
Guatemala	Guatemala	(gwah-tay-MAH-luh)

Glossary

continents (KON–tih–nents)
Most of the land areas on Earth are divided up into huge sections called continents. Guatemala is on the continent of North America.

fiestas (fee–YES–tas)
Fiestas are parties and festivals. There are many different fiestas that are celebrated in Guatemala.

ladinos (lah–DEE–noz)
Ladinos have both Spanish and Mayan relatives. Many Guatemalans are ladinos.

marimba (mah–RIM–buh)
A marimba is a musical instrument that looks a lot like a xylophone. Marimbas make smooth, beautiful music.

plantation (plan–TAY–shun)
A plantation is a large farm where crops are raised. Many different things are grown on Guatemala's plantations.

tortillas (tor–TEE–yas)
Tortillas are flat pancakes that are made of corn or flour. Guatemalans use tortillas in many dishes.

tourism (TOOR–ih–zem)
The business of showing travelers around a country is called tourism. Tourism is a growing business in Guatemala.

Index